CURARE

LUCIAN MATTISON

POETRY

C&R Press
Conscious & Responsible

ISBN 978-1-949540-36-9
LCCN 2022942500

C&R Press
Conscious & Responsible
crpress.org

For special discounted bulk purchases, please contact:
C&R Press sales@crpress.org
Contact info@crpress.org to book events, readings and author signings.

CURARE

CONTENTS

Umbilical

All wilderness
arrives unwieldy,

a fish beaten
against rock. What's left
is nothing

more than a form
of beauty, acceptance
of discomfort

in human
imposition—everything

electrical desert,
ablutions, and barcodes—
nature no longer

completely nature.
Returning is never so
simple as winding

the umbilical
like a garden hose.

Will ages and age
is willing to concede
to this motion.

Teeth sinking
into the belly
of a smaller creature,

I'll never accept or forget
my life is only evidence

of one larger wade
of mother
out into the world—

the instant I break
skin, a dolphin fin
appears, glides

a shallow arc on the edge
of her consciousness.

Uncle

Budapest, Spring

Gripped strollers and cigarettes outside the Dohanybolt,
these mothers' lungs puff, three guardian angels above
infant heads. It's a conversation I can't comprehend.

The silk curtain licks neo-baroque through a window above.
My pregnant sister closes the pane. The child inside
moves as her, is packed pickled eggplant in a glass jar.

A block of compressed ears and limbs, even the idea
of her son is upside down. And just days later,
his wet nose touches sunlight for the first time, listening

to what he has left behind—mother's heartbeat. The father crosses
the Danube in his glass and metal jar, sings to himself
as if in a bubble, a parked muffle of bass and treble.

As parents, they act so many ways except starkly unprepared.
My sister tells me she thinks she can feel her uterus shrink
as she breastfeeds, not sure if what she feels is real.

The child is at peace, eyes closed, tuned to her
inside. I place my hand over my chest, touch the flow of heat
inside, another kind of jarred spirit leaning

on a woman just to fall asleep. Before Budapest, I cut a love
short because I wanted a kid. Or was it the idea of one?
I see her point, more and more—my wants pinned fabric

on a dress form. Remove needles and what looks
like clothing falls, turns inside out at the waist.
Back home, everything wants to fold over itself, expose

the unfinished underside. I am more scared now of what
I thought I've always wanted. It's a natural impulse,
I tell myself, and that's precisely the problem.

Décimas for the Patron Saint of Dogs

San Roque, saint somehow summoned
when my breath was pulled out like red
pepper placenta from my chest,
hollowed on my walk home. The mutts
aggressed, imposed their dominance
and I was just pith, soft matter,
embarrassment of seeds scattered
across butcher block, raised elbows,
chanting his holy name and *no*,
as I was taught by my mother.

Tongue to the wound, a verbal salve,
he didn't drive the dogs away.
I was to be toyed with, weak prey.
Now, I sweep these seeds with the back
of a knife, little pale coins, flat
blade pushing like a penny falls.
Piles of these tokens hanging on,
I hear *death is inside the broom*
scrape across wooden globe, high noon
of fears that amass and totter

on razor's edge. Bristles gather
souls like clumps of dried hair from tiles.
A nest of ticks bite below eyes,
hang like tears from sick dogs. I'm sure
the patron abandoned our world,
bunched white cloth swaddling the bones
in his tomb. I chant, *San Roque*,
San Roque, but the threats don't leave.
What good was he? I tap his teeth,
insist like rain on a window.

Dear saint, if there's ever a time,
it is now. Our world seeks to snuff

out the flickering wick of us.
Perhaps, I'll pray to the canine,
keep the animal at my side
instead, its deft nose leading us.
It licks death with charity's tongue,
licks the earth's canvas until oils
fade to beige, the mutt, so loyal,
licking itself to exhaustion.

Trucker

He says to the truck stop stray
dog, *somos todos bichos, bicho*. He knows

he's the bee, flower a diesel engine—
extinction and exhaust indistinguishable

from the cost of labor. Tio Mario grew up
a pig farmer before driving. As a kid,

he caught bats in nets strung from chicken wire
and branches. He'd hold a creature's face out

like a holy cross to his cousins—*San Roque,*
San Roque, que esos niños no me toquen.

They lit cigarettes, fit a filter between
the creature's little mouth to make it smoke.

Every bat's breath was a fury.
That was childhood, field ecologist

pouring old engine oil onto good earth
and drinking the groundwater below.

Some things are best left behind. Jobs
are redefined. A semi-truck watches

its driver beat his wings like two wipers
against the torrential rain. The blind

do not unionize against sound
logic. A giant hand reaches in, clips a wilted

flower—*no quepan los insectos*, bat navigating
in echoes. Smoking hulk pipes through

the night on auto-pilot. And the driver, side-
saddle to its replacement, hangs by the ankle

from the exhaust like a wet flag,
looks down at a sky full of stars below him.

Remnant

Hands burn under the tap stubborn
grip on a plate   Turning it ice
cold I recoil   in an instant of false searing

perceived error but not   an accident I was
built to avoid pain yet something
                    about inflicting

feels like relief   I peel away the accent
mark of a scab   It's not pleasure
I thumb thin webbing of loose

skin from my greedy mouth's burnt roof
        It rolls along my fingertip
thin scrolls of me   my thousands of layers

       lick raw gum behind teeth
My mass is just this
stacks of film—my eyes are just those

asleep in a hot bath   Take the length of me
peeled   laid flat like a wet handkerchief
drying on tile wall   Sewn into a quilt

how sad that my entirety is only enough
to fill a doorway   I am making light
of that which tens of thousands of years did not

The deep-sea fish won a transparent head
so it now looks   straight through
itself   to find another in darkness

What have we won   that doesn't hurt
us? We are yards   of cobbled
boundaries   Time pales our genetic burdens

shoulders warmed by the work of flake blades
remnants hostile to our own   skin even
though it's everything that encases us

Bulls

I am dreaming up ideal ways to die—
so privileged my entire life—
no practicing the bleakest version
after the bar,
in the ride share,
key in hand at my front door,
or even with the person I've invited inside—
my masculine cloak
the warning stripe
painted across a shark's back.

There's a much more common story.
It repeats and I don't
have to play it out each time.
A woman in a field of bulls
shed her red dress
like a muleta when she saw
she was surrounded by horns.
It doesn't take much imagination
to finish the story.

The next day, townsfolk demand
the rancher bring a gun,
rest the barrel in the culpable
bull's mouth.
He and beast
will only think of food
until the shot. Nobody feels better,
but it is blood.
It paints the grass below us,
again and again,
while the other bulls paw dirt,
sniff the metallic air.

Loophole

Asylum for obsession
to own to choose to take

a life   take cover
under a church pew

become kneeler
below bullet spray   to fight

                    fear with fear is terror
to return fire is   terror to take

death's hand   cold muzzle
the accusing finger

terror   a loophole   takes aim
points toward a body

always   him whites
of eyes pierced by two trembling bullets

so nothing is done   remember
people kill people so guns kill guns triggers

kill triggers so fingers
          interlock   to pray

the rest of one's life kneeling
with eyes open   is terror

is nothing being done
asylum is a roof in a church

refuge   from those we keep
choosing to protect   the pulled trigger

on a loop   again the final rounds
before turning on itself

Curare

Fingers to neck I touch

                    a sound like future

tense—*I*   *will cure you*—

      a promise A pulse

               relaxes into submission

In the left hand

a smaller dose to ease

         suffering   in the right

                 I hold an arrow

poison to pierce push lungs

        into listless amnesia

               A fine line

      between death and healing

and none of us looks well

            From scavengers

we became fisherman

      who stopped in the graveyard

to divide the night's

catch   *One for me*   *One for you*—

      our children only see silhouettes

    among headstones

          believe us

to be God and the Devil dividing souls

before the end—

      One for me

         One for you

Baskets replete we cast

      more lines   empty the reef

    keep the fire lit

stir poison pot

Inhaling a world now overdosed
                I summon a snow-
                                flecked blackbird
        who stoops

        presses its beak to my lips
                        in a dream   It spits
chewed liana vines
                saliva from a clairvoyant

swirls alkaline   around the tongue's
                wet bassinette

                                It arrows down
        the spine, a ray of nerves

like bristling wool rubs static
                        beneath skin

                        Too long speaking to God
we leave the ground
                        deaden the eyes
                of the animal kingdom

Now I offer: take this   this is my body
                reduced to holy prescription

                a bright red resin
        painted on the skin
                to remind me that

                        we are the fire
that we must put out
        and at once
                        are in bed with the flame

The last shaman   who treats living-
                              dead sickness
is about to be buried
          with his medicines and magic

              I pray cure us
          or just be done with the deed

                         In our right hand
                         there is the weight
                              of the world
In the other
the world is a bot
fly in the night
                              almost floating in a web
               The silk orb shakes
                         with electricity of wings
          as a spider
                    wraps it in linen bandages

spins the globe
          like a mummified heart
                         on an axis
still beating

As Light

Flecks of starlings peck pieces from a fried wing
on the asphalt by the driver's side door.
A black tourniquet of beaks in the church lot,
they tug skin, gorge themselves on bird.
I tie the yellow warning flag above the knee
of a discarded church pew, bulk of weight
like legs hung out the back of my pickup truck.
A row of seats given new life on my living room floor,
my guests are a banquet of feet during a party,
the area rug this dusty wooden kneeler. At night,
I recline nude on its long cushion, a figure study
in blasphemy. I make it a point to have sex on its length
because it saddens me as much as it excites.
It took this much drift to see God was always the drunk
driver. He was night, then crumpled
chassis and rubber streaks on pavement. Lights on,
the houses on the block watch an accident
with open windows. He's the harrowing of birds,
orb of flock against the skyline curling black
helices and spheres of starlings. They murmur
meaning out of collective movement, the loss
of life and self. I rest my head on the deadened shoulder
of the divine to fall asleep and my arm goes numb.
The ribcage puffs out before angel wings
are placed on a wooden beam and amputated.
It's what I want to feel—something between
feathers and abandon, something as light
as baked loaves in a basket—against all these odds.

[clouds]

yes tomorrow   is easy today

the reluctant landscape   or does it yield

flaws of perspective? some fine day   we will try

    to do as many things as are possible

        and perhaps we shall succeed

          at all of them

    no longer a promise   the edges

of the image   creep outside the borders   of canvas and we stretch

    the canvas   over more pine

to accommodate that outline

    which precedes us

        *

this togetherness   in still life   projection

    of a salvaged self   narcissist

in its solitude made us

          this way

        there is no longer any harbor

of the self and yet   we are

    all bobbing as if moored

        *

no secrets fill   a drowsy whale

    hollow gullet

its song only　　　speculation　music
its only meaning　　tiny bubbles
escape from the trapped beer　　cask of its baleen

　　　the surface draws　　this small air
magnetized　　　to bubble skin
　　　　it holds nothing in
but the image of being　　　filled　　no center other
　　than the problem born within itself

　　　　　　*

we keep awake like atmosphere　　and clouds　odd
　　　because our heads are the error
in the code

　　and I thought differently
　　and I thought differently

here is the wind that gives up

before the sail　retreats backward
　　　　away from the billow's pull
almost　　living the assonance
　　　　　　of accidents
　　Ashbery a fisheye
　　fastened to happenstance　　What good
is the line without　　hook or
　　　　　　sinker　our future

just rows of cirrus like ploughed earth

21

its comprehension only   as important as its fruit

*

the present margins a cloud   falls away
     whispered around
the atmosphere   it ends up identical to what
     was never intended   after hours
of explanation   only our end is what matters
to those who were   never any help whatsoever

     opposite hand the extent of knowledge
thoughts are miles   above us   unpracticed
     scrawling names in chalk
     on the big blue   each letter
     with wings drawn

Different Gravity

Curl of a wave, entireties swallowed, swell
after swell, I'm in a giant nervous body

of water—a step into surf, on oyster blade,
something alive. A claw squeezes,

hurts just enough that I pull up my foot
as if from hot metal. On one crab's back, the ocean

transforms into one giant organism—
sea floor crawling with segmented legs,

each crustacean a wandering nerve
ending—me, a neural fire in the axon, a dull pain

stood on two feet. Up to my chest in the endless,
careless steps amid the toss, I jar

this moonwalk, one more animal leaving its feet
in a different gravity. Pelicans splash

into chopped wake. Wings spread, the birds
beat air, a brief violence before folding

into a bobbing drop of oil on the water's
warming surface. A whole world of warnings

follow this smooth curve. A globe will eventually
come to rest after the disorder of us. The ebb tide

rubs away the shell's edge. I put my foot down
again onto the wet sheet of universe,

the broken pieces of life preceding me, millions
atop more millions, at once, underfoot.

Apocapolyptych with Sea Nettles

Your image is beached
on my temporal lobe.

I am up to my waist
in the ocean. The strings
of your lappets
send vibrations through
the warming water, as I wade

in the current,
retreat at the thought
of wrapping myself with your body.

§

You cannot pull your eyes away
from the bell jar of my head,
meters of tentacle
reaching back toward the ocean.

In the open air, I'm a deflated object.
Sea foam clings to my hood
like rope tethering a glass float.

I only weigh as much as the seawater
that you pour into my head.

§

Sitting side by side,
we talk about the Pacific

24

sea nettle beached feet from us.

We pluck wet fronds
from kelp stipes
and bind one another's legs.

I hear my spirit rattle
in your head, a previous version
of me knocking.

Your nude figure rolls
along the inside of my skull
like the tongue of a bell.

§

In one version of this, it is much later.
We are both sea nettles
washed up on shore.

Your limp body is carried
someplace else in a gull's beak.

I am just a memory strewn
in gelatinous pieces along the coast.

§

This morning, I partitioned
the idea of us
into dumb objects, so as not to see

a broken whole.
Whitewater tumbles at my feet,

lifts the floating signifier,
so many possibilities receding into surf.

This is how we all disappear:

you're ankle deep on a sandbar,
hundreds of feet
offshore, and you ask me
to walk toward you.

Husks

Tethered to a signpost
a dog runs circles so long
it becomes butter
outside the café

Tio Hugo holds bread
in one hand
rakes the pat with a knife
says the dog
evolved leashed

a miniscule yellow
wave of fat curls
hides the blade

                    *

                              though he can't express it
                         tio became a traveling street clown
                         in Spain because it was the only way
                                   he felt safe in drag

                                        in a crowd
                                     she's a horny nun
                                        next day
                                    a beautiful dunce
                                   a clumsy little girl

                                  every woman he loves
                                    to be and away

                                  from every woman
                                    who raised him

                                        often growth in another
                                        direction seems enough

                                        as if stretching toward sun
                                        I see him and I'm not sure
                                                      what is fixed?

                                *

expired Christs pile up
wail in the kitchen sink
if thorns cut my hand
as I clean wounds
that's my problem

I fill a glass with water
because it is meant to carry it
I fill it with soil and still
water makes it in

the three sprouts
on my windowsill hold up
their seed husks to the light
like Kodachrome slides

everything they are becoming
was packed inside them to start
crumb of an obsession
that begins and ends
in the same place

                                *

                                        so much for growth

                              the countless contracts
                              we never had the chance

                                    to opt out of
                              branches extend outward
                                in a crown of shade
                               structures that mock
                      the absurdity in the smallness
                                      of a seed

                              machista reaches down
                            like roots grips masculine
                                  soil my culture
                              I spade and press down

                            the endless subconscious
                                 listens for water
                                rain flicks wet tap
                          of neural liquid slides over
                                  the tilt of leaves
                        sprouted plinko pins that drop us
                                around the trunk
                                 to beckon roots

                                        *

after a year away from home
I dream of Union Station
under renovation
great hall vault blanketed in white cloth
walls the scaffolded molt
of mantis skeleton

the desirous mind waits
to get picked up
if it wishes it can terrify itself

or summon a version of who it loved
maybe both

the lack of choice
in how it throws me
predicts perfection outside
the constellations painted
on the curved roof
of the skull

locked into binaries it is both
poison and a cure
in these stations

sometimes we are left
more often than not
we are left in the dark

*

Though there isn't a need
Tio Hugo is performing
a different role
takes me to an Argentinean steak house
talks about hot women and soccer
orders entraña flat gold chain
sits against a hairless chest

I believe this act
like I believe his hair is still brown
mid-sixties and he still can't
go home

I'm family
word could get back
the rigidity

makes me want to nail the idea
of man onto the beam
and let it suffocate

*

I am so much more than this
husk silken beard and stalks
I delight in my completeness
a whole body lowered into water
measured in what is displaced

the brain brims ecstatic spill
over the lips
masculine physicality
this buzzing thing somehow separate
from me and only me at once

submerged in a hot bath
almost weightless
there is so much outside of the body
I wash my present tense
run hands over every piece
of organic purpose as reminder

how I start to the simple and stark
eroticism of human
a tendon stalk pulled taught
up the thigh
by bent knees
a hip bone
slopes down into continental shelf
subducted plate
boiling ocean and the tongue
is a mammal in the strobe
of filtered sunlight

a lover swims around a sunken statue
of what once was
man's likeness
nude turned teeming reef

[clouds]

under a black umbrella   the cheek is a subway

map of lines printed   across the face

by pillows   folded up and shaken fabric

then underground

half asleep   against the train window

what seem   like rain clouds

float along the inside

of closed eyes   our world inside

the smallest device   a cloud of information

shuttled invisibly   this decade will be different

because everything appears the same around us

spit out at a different stop   rain pricking the ground

except for a rip in the canvas

stretched across segmented metal

skeleton   overhead   it drips

incessantly on the screen   and the clouds do not

relent   they never will

Infinite Sharks

Your shark will become a different shark
when you enter a new town, lie

back to the birds and branches
painted on the tiles of the baptismal font.

After a year waist deep in the water,
your pants will have disintegrated

and you'll be a nude prune bathing
during church service hours, host

to a procession of scolding looks
as the bells chime everyone from inside.

You will stand up, genitals flailing,
and declare that you've killed

that basin's shark, that its stuffed cavity
is on display in the local museum,

jaw removed and mounted to a doorway
so townsfolk can pass through

simulating the act of being eaten alive.
The collection basket will circulate.

You'll remove your hat, bow,
and move on to the next town

stopping for new pants along the way,
a stray dog following you like a saint.

You will sell the same dead shark
as many times as you can, each under

a different name, and the hope is
someday collection baskets

will be abolished, museums chock-full,
and sharks infinite. Then your shark

will no longer be a shark, but a hunger
will remain in the water. Another year

will shovel clouds onto our coffin's
glass lid. Through the ceiling

of overcast, you'll just make out
the outline of a giant creature—*San Roque,*

San Roque, que este bestia no me toque.
A larger, stranger beast stoops,

lowers its lips into our atmosphere,
and opens its mouth to drink.

Moon Landing

Flattening dozens of pint-size
snowmen beneath a boot's
rubber tread, I wish

I really was that large,
cataclysmic, as bad at math
as Calvin, unloosed as Hobbes.

I chalk proofs for nothing at all
on the blackboard, so much
erased to shades of dust

clouds, it's like I'm sketching
the Milky Way. After decades
of detention, me and hundreds

of dads across the world agree
everybody should quit
looking for other planets

to inhabit, but what's Spaceman
Spiff without those cancerous blobs
raising Martian pitchforks

overhead?—a drunk pilot
aimlessly floating through space.
For him, each crash and razor-

thin escape is enough to erase
speculation over something
so rudimentary in comparison—

walking on the moon—
enough to ease concerns
about the integrity of that lunar

lander's gold foil shell
separating the astronaut
from the infinite quiet

by just a pencil tip. So, we agree,
it wasn't conspiracy. Now, let's solve
something more meaningful

before we let us drown our world.
Otherwise, someone shut us
inside a cardboard box

labeled *time machine*,
tape the flaps down, and rock us
until we are children again.

Then, all we will see above us
are slits of light in the shape
of a cross. It's a beautiful heap

of horseshit, but I'd want back in
if I could believe in so fantastic
a world again. This planet

will be as desolate
as the surface of the moon,
radiant globe where I boot

footballs across tracts of the nothing
we call a pitch, where I coexist
with satellites and robot rovers

worshipping the clouds
like a bunch of sluggish pagans,
ground where I plant seedlings

in what feels like the earth's ashes

after fire, the past and future
spilling from between my fingers.

After Burning Down My Hoarder Uncle's House

We're both wanted men
but none of us knows it just yet.

I've looked at you differently
ever since you told me:

*I'd rather it all burn to the ground
than begin to clean up this mess I've made.*

Maybe you didn't mean it, but I did.
If it all would just disappear,

I could start over too.
What would you do if I chose to save

cartons of milk just because
their expiration dates

were like birthdays, stockpiled
newspapers, textbooks, and dented cans

like Doric ruins in my living room,
rewrote the true gospel

so I could save nobody's soul,
nor a cent for retirement?

How many decades must pass
before we can see you again?

I burned it all down just to know
how your eyes bobbed outside

the fishbowls of your lenses; it burned
so I could pull out your circuitry

by the handful, until your towering frame
was almost weightless. The past is

in wet piles and charred rubble.
You would have done the same for me.

Church Retreat

The folk singer
tears from a loaf
of rustic bread, leather-

bound lyric books
brimming with spirituals
in our hands.

He thrums strings,
almost unwittingly,
as the breadbasket

moves from hand
to hand. We rip
chunks, fill our mouths

with this shrinking
lump of crust,
a handful of kids left

passing crumbs,
possibly a lesson to come.
He sings an elegy,

harmonies that pine
for the one
from our past

never touched, kissed,
or eclipsed—
that far off love

and God,
interchangeable. Everyone

looks from the page

to the sky, anywhere
but toward the ground,
as if paradise

were far away
on a strange world
other than our own.

Super Saturday

What we thought was cold
two months ago, now,
carves stream melt
through ploughed piles of snow,
rill trickling downhill
along the blanketed curb
like an underground river.
In the laundromat, machines
hum, roll their little red eyes
and damp, blue cotton
blends, and on the TV Trump
is now a full-blown speaker
box, granite teeth
spreading across his face.
Pale as the obelisk's tip,
he pierces low hanging clouds
with an expanding head.

Watching my clothing tumble
in circles, I can't help but feel
we will be duped again.
We try to mark what he does not
say—the magician
uses only one hand, speaks and signs
with the other. It's all farce
until we see our number
in red diamonds in his fingers, in disbelief
that we wouldn't miss
the small moment
where it all happened,
hook on which no bait was hung.

Wet clothes lump
at the bottom of the washer's porthole
like an unspilled tear,

and the morning news program
slings empathy over the branch
of an oak. Tied to the other end
of the rope is a bucket,
brimming with fresh water,
sloshing over our heads.
Pundits are talking
about this country's thirst
and how relief is within reach,
while we're all left to consider
how we would maneuver
in a world where in place of our faces,
neighbors see large white mouths
on ravenous bodies, lips
to the dirt, burying ourselves.

Floe Pastoral

He watches a polar bear scratch its back
on a tuft of snow, as seals
slurp in and out of arctic water.

There's also a place nearby
with only one hole in the ice for miles.

A desperate seal presses nose to frozen
ceiling or bleeds from batted
flanks between breaths, bear

paw fur flecked red. The bear just waits
for the inevitable to surface.

And weeks are spent sleeping
on leaves of ice sheets.
It hears the crackle,

fear overwritten by hunger.
This plays out on a television,

bears afloat on tiny private islands—
the temperature of the Arctic Ocean?
Fucking cold, okay.

Which ape, head draped
with a cloth napkin, keeps ordering ortolan

for dinner? His chef strikes
a match, lights the pilot.
He holds the recognizable world

with pedaling feet over the pot,
the whole house a billow of gas

and brandy. And the bears
on screen slink into the midnight blue,
can only chase their next meal.

It's a Party

You've been invited to another party inside the stomach
of a tiger, and this time you have no excuses.

You're between TV shows, that depression that is
procrastinating within the act of procrastination,
so the tiger's stomach starts to sound like an okay idea:

warmth, a host of other people making out
their names among each table's blood-stained tent cards,

tapas, and sangria. You've stopped going outside
because everyone is angry at you, thinks you prefer avocado puree
over shelter, nihilism over ignorance. Aren't you embarrassed

you've never shot a gun, let alone held one?
How can you take away their right to access mass murder

having never mass murdered yourself? Lots of people
are upset that you think they need to die
before any significant change occurs in the country.

Death to them is not a formality, but more like somebody
lighting their money and clothes on fire. Dress code for the party

is formal. You wear tiger print, put on a paper tiger
headdress. You look out at a world framed by teeth.
Children are not allowed, so people will complain

about your phone instead. *PUT IT AWAY, IT'S A PARTY.*
Six times during the night your boss calls.

Four times you explain how to digitally sign PDFs
with food in your mouth. You and the internet
are mostly to blame for everyone's problems.

Every so often, the dancefloor in the middle of the tiger stomach
turns into a hole and people fall in mid-shimmy.

Bruno Mars is the last thing they hear before they die.
You put up your feet, rest them atop the remaining patatas
bravas and white anchovies. You are going to die this way,

and people are just starting to loosen up after the third round
of champagne. The tiger drapes itself over a branch.

It spends 80% of its life asleep. That seems preferable
to constantly being told, by those same people who hate you,
how to fix your life and what to buy in order to do so.

They're scared because they need you to survive.
They always have. They throw these parties to keep tabs on you.

They like that you ask everyone around you for forgiveness,
though you don't know what it is you've done wrong
that wasn't asked of you to begin with. It's become a kind of ritual.

The tiger's purrs reverberate up the stomach lining. The guests
cheer. It's still a party, they didn't lie. It *is* warm inside.

[clouds]

paperless

        between

which flowers are

      pressed/voice/pressed

between silences

        everyone

is everyone's biographer

we illuminate

      in a screen's blink

mock shutter

speed unprecedented

Basement

Sometimes it's like the couple above
dropped a handful of marbles

of all sizes on the floor. Pieces
of their universe expand and roll on my ceiling,

    radiate from a wooden singular

        point. A heel
strikes linoleum, accompanied by clicks
of untrimmed dog nails—the animal

barks incessantly, dumbest dog alive
tethered to the kitchen overhead

like a balloon in the wind.

      I try not to hate this animal,
pointless as it is
           by no fault of its own.
It whines neglect among muffled
arguments, frustration an ungreased pulley

climbing
    and descending musical scales. After dinner
    there is sleep. Morning

    presses down, coffee grounds lodged
in the gaps of teeth. I rise twelve feet below them

as if from the grave, mouth agape, here

with the occasional cricket,
house centipede, spider—sleep rolled away

from the eyes like heavy granite.

The unmade bed

      is a swirl of flattened blades of grass,
damp under upturned stone.

I recognize the darkness that surrounds
their absence above,
         cold out for a stroll
before light, rats tire-smashed in the alleyway
                  and frozen over,

      walking atop the ice flat of blood
and water. I am still so young
              and what plays out

above me is tired, frightening.
           A skeleton folds
        over itself at the foot

of the mausoleum's door after days
of beating a stone door.

I keep a quartered orange in my mouth,
             teeth penned on
my nutrition.

      I don't want desperation
to bead on the windows, to work until death,
      live inside the creaks

of a ghost's footsteps overhead,
another read-through of scripted roles
         at the round table,
    eyes awash in early hours.

I'm already handing over every last cent

to this city. So, death keeps demanding—
                              nickel clink
                 in her pocket, as if she walks

         just beyond the basement wall,
the soil parting for her like curtains.

Paper Wasp

The cabin window overlooks a thicket
of scrub brush, pine and saw palms.
I left a lover. Sprawled on a new mattress,
I've found something I had forgotten
went missing, but this time it fails
to surprise me: paper wasp embalmed
in the eaves, beam of dust flecks cutting across
the room in a constant state of rising,
sheets bunched at the foot of an empty bed.
So, this is the freedom I desired so much—
wilderness devoid of animals,
hidden in the snowfall of ashes
from a nearby brush fire. I left her
and a few odd belongings behind
in a city apartment for every right reason.
I just opened the door and she is already waiting
for me to come back for them.

Saturday Morning

Two fingers rest on the soil's
shoulder, pepper pot watered into a bloom
of coffee grounds.

A generous portion floods
the plate below,
while the mind dredges itself in flour,

powder of maladies we keep rolling in
our heads. Soaked earth

weighs, roots grip dirt as if sewn on.
I don't ask anything more of the world

because it is tired from resisting
all we pull.
If it remembers me a sprout in a bowl

of dirt, my thanks overflow—gratitude
a fuel that burns infinitely,

if I just let it. See
how the soil drinks from its plate
like a good cat?

All that is sour in me is a drop
on the tongue. It's embarrassingly light.

I twist the row of blinds, pull the sun
out from between the slats.
It covers everything in columns

of warmth, in more cosmic things
I cannot see. I cannot fathom.

Office Pastoral

Clutched barbed wire   two eyelids
stretched open,
exit the iris   onto tilled earth.

Wind deleaves me
like an artichoke.   Without coat
for the cold, I make home

in the mule's ear. They call me
two things: tasked, defective—
tighten   the leather saddle.

A burden whispers in the ear,
        debtless dream populated
by loaves and fish,   five more

miracles, minimum,   please.
Was this a promotion? I pass stemmed
champagne   flutes with a hoof

        (they drop).   Birds collect
the pieces, nest between my ears
in confusion.   So many hours

thrown into a lake of rent   learning
to fish   is laughable.
The office hosts another party

with games.   The creature leans
        its flank into the fence barbs,
pins itself   to itself.

[clouds]

there was a specific time
when my phone and a pigeon
      held about equal value

now I grip one like rope   that threads
a piton driven into sheer cliff face

mountain of information   clouds

a drifting landscape below me
as I hold on
      for dear life   at dinner

my greatness is two minds:
      operator frantically plugging cables
      into a switchboard   and a trivia champion

my partner and I
      place ourselves face-down
         on a table

         conversation divided
into quarters like orange slices
as the night's text

threads fill like helium balloons
beg us to look   where

there are two of us   there are actually six
all speaking at the same time

                        like it or not

I'm in this   kind of   oversoul
                we've always wished for

                but most of the time
it sounds like a mix   of chimes

auto insurance ads and the Jurassic
Park theme played
          on a plastic recorder   the right hand

          and pocket
are beacons   attached to us

a clubbed foot
        stepping through a cloud

and nobody is happy
        about falling until
              we see we
        actually
fall forward

Dino DNA

I want to emulate the timbre
      of Dennis's squeal,
how a can of Barbasol
      triggers desire to clone millions
of years in a single sound.
      Is this the contemporary
poet—goat tethered to a pole,
      idea of Tyrannosaurus
lurking in a static rainforest?

      At my best, I'm Dr. Ian Malcolm
dipping his finger in a plastic cup.
      I drip beads onto a woman's hand,
whisper a theory for this falling
      water into her ear, everything
tumbling away from the tip
      of her knuckle.

But most days acting the scholar
      seems as if it's only a matter
of sticking around long enough
      to be suffocated
in the resin of a tree.
      I need a drop of blood,
blueprint to build a living thing,
      frog DNA to fill in the holes.

As far as I can remember,
      I have been trying to clone
everyone that has come
      before me, let the lawyer inside
perish in the mouth
      of a lizard—me, the toilet
that collects storm water,
      palm fronds in a pile around me.

The world continues to wave
        a stick in the face
of an indifferent reptile,
        asks it to fetch. I'm told *No*
wonder you're extinct, as my teeth
        are pushed out by those
of a crocodile, my open frill
        a night-bloom amid the chaos.

Tiger

I am too elevated a creature
to drool so profusely.
Nose on yellow-streaked
pillow, half out the case
like a calf tongue,
I'm roused hunger and disgust
at my time spent in bed.
Head, as if suspended
on a meat hook, ogles, dumb,
desperate, lowest
denominator of brute—
wears the same expression
for sleep, sex, and observing
the sedentary life of spiders
marooned in the ceiling lights.
Rolled in a sheet like sheep's
clothing, I witness my wants
reduce to syrup.
A tiger inside licks its teeth,
paces the aisle
of this commercial jet,
demands to see the pilot
behind the voice.
Even the crew fastens
their seatbelts, eyes cast
on the big cat as it noses
pant legs and carry-ons.
The cockpit door opens.
The pilot scratches the beast
under the chin, ushers it inside.
With a heavy jolt, it takes control
of the vessel, aims upward.

[clouds]

many unalike full

        as a closed hand

    that grabs at a gnat

   swarm   the palm

opens in expectation

        of beating

wings a fist

    that hums   nothing

    truly empty

    yet obsessed by

        the idea—is empty

      a virtue?

a landscape

    within the loose cage

    of fingers populated

by leaves of sweat

flat density

        of wild the hand

again snatches

at the humming cloud

trying to grab a hold

of anything I am

                a needle desirous

for magnetic north

            nose always trained

on the unbuffered space

                        on a map

        for fulfillment found

in the unknown

        does our circumnavigation

always arrive at

                the back of the head?

            the sun taps us

                    on the shoulder

and we turn and answer

        to the authority of morning

            we sail east

to see if the sun

is an insect

we can pinch

with two fingers

cycling legs pulled

from the sea

and seagulls

follow the trawler

swooping chevrons

the shallow arcs

of their falling

stitching together melody

Subject in Subject

At this age, let's call a heart a spade,
the previous night's clothes, dry leaves.

Drunkard sweeps the tiles with death's broom—
dust, hair, tags—evidence

of existence in piles next to my shoes.
There are large holes in the story,

a shark-proof cage with a panel missing.
I'm overtly host to something else's meaning,

fearing the bacteria alive inside my viscera
more than the worms that will blossom,

burst forth from the bloat of body.
Saying *no* to the smell, *okay* to aging and *no*

to waiting, I touch colder skin
to prove to myself that I still fill it, pat

the dog peeking through the neighbor's gate
to be sure the sidewalk doesn't roll on its side.

A morning routine scours clues,
scratches letters into little boxes

that make up hosts of bigger boxes.
I darken the ghosts of letters as the grid

of unknowns spill outward into the known,
a rare opportunity to declare

that these spaces we inhabit aren't anything
but exactly what they're supposed to be.

Trickster

These are a carnivore's
fingers stubborn

with hunger. Cone collars
fastened to both my wrists,

large one around the neck,
and I'd still be that anxious

dog, bite the one spot
I shouldn't, chase the rabbit

down the hole. The plucked
patch in my beard grows,

my face a peach
with a bite missing,

and I'm still hard at work
digging around for the ingrown

culprit, fully aware
I'm going about it all wrong.

Isn't this what we are
actually taught—relief

only a matter of trying
harder, doing more

even if it means bleeding
in the process? Rabbit, a promise

that someday we won't need
patience and a turpentine baby

but to keep digging.
We can always feel it

on our fingertips,
the exception we might be

to the paths beaten before us,
how in the next moment

the whole forest could be
in awe as we trot off

in the opposite direction,
trickster caught limp in the jaw.

Asleep atop Bed Bugs

Nightly, the box
spring sweats dark drops
of insects, each one
a ripe polyp of black raspberry,
skins taut to the cusp
of rupture. My bed
has become a bottle
of polluted laborers,
my skin the soil
of an ancient earth.
Mounds rise like incense ash—
the remnants of prayers
on my skin in cold
welts. Generations
have worshipped. A nocturnal
pilgrimage to my body
is all some know.
I try to speak the language
of our universe,
but increase the scale
and stars fall like dice
in the night sky.
It's only now that I understand
the urge to abandon
those who have nothing else
but the silent weight
of a larger presence
pressing down on them—
how we were all left
on this earth.

In Rafflesia

Slide on a long sleeve and leave
camp at twilight to catch sunrise—arrive

to earth crowning over rarest flora.
Sabah is any rainforest in the dark,

thick with insect prattle. Tread a path,
carve herbage out with two hands.

Slip on fungi, sink to your ankles
in alluvial soil, as movements

of small nature seep tropical nutrients
into your socks. Heed odor

of florescence, carrion flower's spathe,
dank raffle plump with microbial

bloat and beetles—mammalian
music to flies. You'll be lucky

to see this three-foot blossom,
twenty-pound bulk surprisingly shy

in a bank of dirt, petals like leather,
rubicund and spotted white.

The corolla gapes a yawn
as if waking from lifelong sleep.

In Rafflesia's beak see the moon
mouthing silent instructions   bud nine

months, blossom three days,
host a rancid buffet for the insects.

Envy the longevity of a mayfly: its birth
a rarity in bloom, lifetime spent

in the opulence of petals, death
a harmony to waning aromas.

To stay is to drink silence of toxic fruits,
humbled by the eternity of plants—

years never more trivial next to this
flower. It blooms, returns to the earth

a devotion as fervent as any string
of prayers murmured into clasped hands,

faith emerging like silk from a spider.
On the trees hang clusters of pitchers.

They offer little champagne flutes, afloat
in the humidity. Here is our tenure

among insects—to take a glass,
grasp the pitfall trap of coniine,

to taste rainfall, poison runnel,
and the spill of mountain

air threading your throat with flame,
to lift a ruffled petal, chop off

a hock and bite into the all-
consuming luxury, paralyzed by flowers.

And like that, a more beautiful life
lets its petals fall back to earth,

reclining in sky, a golden stag
beetle's wing rising inside the eyelid.

Fish

So casual the godless
rejoinder to believer.
We temper words,
but not these.
My friend of faith won't
a dram or drop,
the uttered novella
in sober prose—
but how would I answer me
telling myself
I was no longer
completely myself?
And nobody is wrong
about god and, thus,
so much proffered
in the immaculate
peopling of an egg,
little fish of humanity,
lord of all fish. I am
no better or worse
for the hook scar
on my lip,
and somehow
an inexhaustible food
in the right hands.

Cultured Meat Pastoral

Goats and cows' dreams have little pull yet. Cheese
is still cheese, piston driven milkers likely painful. The future

of sirloin strips it of skin, legs, bones, grown without

the cortex of overcast blanketing cow consciousness.

Michelin stars will be reserved for those meals sporting limbic

systems, pain, rich diets—*enough with the classism already*—

the elite restaurant in the country: rusted windmill

atop stack stone, stag rack looms over dark leather, rills

of watery blood flood the soil around the abattoir just beyond

sniffing distance. Even holding the boning knife, I identify

with meat cow, a future of massage and organic feed,

head on the chopping block after so many years heart healthy,

conscience lighter than droplets perched on the bristles

of melon vine. I look out the kitchen window at the coop.

The chickens are so dumb. They dream of dirt

or of nothing at all, steep nightly in complete darkness.

A few of them keep cannibalizing their own eggs. The farmer

instructs to replace them with golf balls so with each peck

at the dimples the hens learn to stop making shitty choices.

I ask the farmer to consider the nugget of lab grown breast

in a drive-thru, the cleaner, friendlier option. Like with hens,

progress is mostly about making the best decision the least

amount of work for everyone or just plain deceiving the public

until it's done. The slaughter is artisanal, boutique a strangled calf.

When it suits the market, we'll remove the brain stem

from food, guilt from consumption. We'll give the cartoon T-bone

steak on the label eyes with which to wink at us—playful way

to stop cannibalizing our world, only when it suits us.

Butcher

A desk job turns me into a domed cake
where before I tapped glass with a fingernail,
always on the outside—*how delicious, expensive.*
Look how I've outdone the expectations
I had set for my absurd self. Now able
to pay rent without skipping meals,
I've had time to develop these new life goals:
buy jamonero for the kitchen counter
loaded with a home-cured ham, ham
knife for the serrano ham, skills enough
to slice ham, paper thin, with one hand.
More ham goals: gout, hosting a ham
themed party, different hams in the ham
closet, artisanal ham-curing dirt pit
in the backyard, dying penniless.
The brain is a monster with many aspirations
massaged into his creases with a carving knife.
I consume my sadness at the expense
of another's life and only bat an eyelash
if it begins to walk on two legs.
I understand my privilege allows me
to wear a cake dome as a helmet
while stargazing on Mars. So, I think I'm happy,
but I want to abandon security
for a new career path curing meats.
New ham goals: use ham leg to kick ball
into back of net, consult shaman
about ham souls and curare, raise a ham
from dead, teach ham knife skills,
hire ham to hang me from a rope
in cool room so I retain moisture
and receive proper ventilation. The ham asks
the necromancer which professions
we consider virtuous—a life dedicated
to curing humans over the keyboard,

not so bad. Knife held above the neck,
it's not the act of cutting away the body
that is noble, it's the butcher— he, who
cleans the blood from the blade, folds
a neat package in his namesake paper.

Upon Not Seeing the Ghosts of a Velociraptor or My Dead Grandmother

Human law perpetuates
this flaw of logic
that reaches into the other-
worldly, disembodied voice
of a shriveled woman,
but never a bird of
prey at the foot of the bed.
If ghosts remain,
then they claim the earth
by numbers and cacophony,
our planet coated in the myelin
of dead things: velociraptor
feathers brush the cheek
of the Great Khan, his left boot
perched on the clasper
of a beached Megalodon,
tens of millions of years
of Cambrian explosion—
diapsid reptiles, coelacanths,
and dorudons—distending
the shark's pale stomach
right outside of a Cocoa
Beach bungalow window.
Think of how many organisms
are dying inside of us
at any given moment,
sinus to colon.
What is considered *finished*
business when there is so much
on this planet left to consume,
so much afterlife
to look forward to? Each night,
I sleep inside a cloud
of thousands of Triassic

mosquitoes, proboscises
the pins and needles
in my arm, numb weight
under my pillow.
I like to think
we are being consumed
by all these ghosts
and this is the reason we age.
And sometimes, I prefer
to imagine nothing at all,
just so I may fall asleep,
all of these spirits in tow, unsure
of how to proceed without me.

Trashcendent

Let's stuff newborn mouths with plastics,
wear 50-gallon trash can liners as furs, zip-tie
disposable dinnerware to the end
of a Swiffer mop spear. Dip palms in an ink pool
of cracked toner cartridges and get handsy
with the inside of a cave wall. Let's swap bloodlogged
organs for lightweight hoses and pouches—lungs
are vacuum bags, liver a distiller's retort.
Pilgrimage is inevitable and the highest form
to which the body aspires. As the Buddha,
printed on yoga mat, instructs: let capitalism
kill itself with speed, let mind be riparian
and float out into the ocean. The self
is the gyre's pull, Pacific garbage patch
the last pristine place. The earth rests its empty head
against the breast of universe, she disposes
of the bodies. We melt into a living collective.
A sea turtle lays eggs in my stomach. Anchovies feed
on the skin of legs wilted toward ocean floor.
Spongy bones are a network of caverns, fill
with salt water and shrimps. Decades of nail growth
curl keratin coral branches over fingers, and my hair
is an endless kelp stipe plumbing the depths,
its slight curve an echo of the earth's rotation.

[clouds]

if there is a god I am becoming it more
and more every day   if there is   a god it is
benevolent   a face lit by the present
tense documenting   I hold reality
as it unspools from a warren
in my palm   I hold
everything   I pocket
everything   I feel stunted without
everything   communion with the nearest cell
tower a thin signal   crossing the blood
brain barrier   we watch from afar
the theater of world   recorded
Even carrying their own cameras officers
do the unspeakable
unapologetic   like gods   we hold
the suffocating   and caged in our hands
replay   so much untouchable
violence floats over   a country through us
like a heavy mist though it smells
of poison   there is a cure within it
we will document this world   into submission
until it eventually feels real again soon
enough   the clouds will hold
everyone accountable
and that is their only promise

Acknowledgements

Grateful acknowledgment is made to the following publications in which some of these poems appeared or will appear:

The 4th River: "Paper Wasp" (previously titled "Single")
The Acentos Review: "Basement," "Subject in Subject," "Umbilical"
Apt: "Asleep Atop bed Bugs"
Bluestem: "Trickster"
Bodega: "After Burning Down My Hoarder Uncle's House"
Hobart: "[clouds] yes tomorrow," "Cultured Meat Pastoral," "Fish"
Interrupture: "Upon Not Seeing the Ghost of a Velociraptor or My Dead Grandmother"
Juked: "Trucker"
MAYDAY: "As Light"
[PANK]: "Remnant"
Prelude Magazine: "[clouds] paperless," "[clouds] if there is a god," "[clouds] there was a specific time"
The Shallow Ends: "Moon Landing"
Sixth Finch: "It's a Party"
Split Lip Magazine: "Apocapolyptych with Sea Nettles" (previously "A Sea Nettle Washes Up"), "Dino DNA"
Sugar House Review: "Office Pastoral"
Third Coast: "Loophole" (Poetry Prize, finalist)
Up the Staircase Quarterly: "Super Saturday"

C&R PRESS TITLES

NONFICTION

This is Infertilility by Kirsten McLennan
Currciulm Viate by Gregory de la Haba
East Village Closed by Billy the Artist
Many Paths by Bruce McEver
By the Bridge or By the River? Stories of Immigration
from the Southern Border by Amy C. Roma
Women in the Literary Landscape by Doris Weatherford, et al
Credo: An Anthology of Manifestos & Sourcebook for Creative
Writing by Rita Banerjee and Diana Norma Szokolyai

FICTION

Juniper Street by Joan Frank
Transcendent Gardening by Ed Falco
All I Should Not Tell by Brian Leung
Last Tower to Heaven by Jacob Paul
History of the Cat in Nine Chapters or Less by Anis Shivani
No Good, Very Bad Asian by Lelund Cheuk
Surrendering Appomattox by Jacob M. Appel
Made by Mary by Laura Catherine Brown
Ivy vs. Dogg by Brian Leung
While You Were Gone by Sybil Baker
Cloud Diary by Steve Mitchell
Spectrum by Martin Ott
That Man in Our Lives by Xu Xi

SHORT FICTION

A Mother's Tale & Other Stories by Kahanh Ha
Fathers of Cambodian Time-Travel Science by Bradley Bazzle
Two Californias by Robert Glick
Notes From the Mother Tongue by An Tran
The Protester Has Been Released by Janet Sarbanes

ESSAY AND CREATIVE NONFICTION

Selling the Farm by Debra Di Blasi
the internet is for real by Chris Campanioni
Immigration Essays by Sybil Baker
Death of Art by Chris Campanioni

POETRY

Curare by Lucian Mattison
How to Kill Yourself Instead of Your Children by Quincy Scott Jones
Lottery of Intimacies by Jonathan Katz
What Feels Like Love by Tom C. Hunley
The Rented Altar by Lauren Berry
Between the Earth and Sky by Eleanor Kedney
What Need Have We for Such as We by Amanda Auerbach
A Family Is a House by Dustin Pearson
The Miracles by Amy Lemmon
Banjo's Inside Coyote by Kelli Allen
Objects in Motion by Jonathan Katz
My Stunt Double by Travis Denton
Lessons in Camoflauge by Martin Ott
Millennial Roost by Dustin Pearson
All My Heroes are Broke by Ariel Francisco
Holdfast by Christian Anton Gerard
Ex Domestica by E.G. Cunningham
Like Lesser Gods by Bruce McEver
Notes from the Negro Side of the Moon by Earl Braggs
Imagine Not Drowning by Kelli Allen
Notes to the Beloved by Michelle Bitting
Free Boat: Collected Lies and Love Poems by John Reed
Les Fauves by Barbara Crooker
Tall as You are Tall Between Them by Annie Christain
The Couple Who Fell to Earth by Michelle Bitting
Notes to the Beloved by Michelle Bitting